To My Mother,

Who never gave up on me,
I love you a buncha grapies.

Love, B.

Waves.

-

They say these types of things
They come in waves
There was the Great Big Flood
And then there was Katrina
But nothing could ever prepare me
For the chaos that was to ensue
The beginning of him
Was the ending of me
The Pine trees bustled in the wind
But even their needles
Never hurt as much
As his

Little White Lies.

-
At first
They said it was the drugs talking
Your little girl knew drugs couldn't speak
How could they?
But the way you left bruises on her mother
The very essence of peace
Was to be gone with the wind
Play dates turned into
Drug runs
Medicine or Skittles?
You can't crush skittles between
Two metal spoons
Can you?
White dust or
White lies?

My First

-
I remember my firsts
First kiss
We were five and six
In the classroom
First heartbreak
I was nine
You broke your
Very first promise to me
You said you'd quit
Smoking
Smoking
Smoking
A habit I was
Far too young
To understand
Turns out
Drugs
Drugs
Drugs
Wasn't the only

Habit
Habit
Habit
I would be
Kicking
Kicking
Kicking
Two decades
Later

Twelve.

-
I was twelve
Scars on my legs and
Cuts up my arms
I was twelve
I counted each cut
Seventy-eight, seventy-nine...
Each cut
One reason to die
I was twelve
You grabbed my arm
Looked at me and said
How
Pathetic
I was twelve
I didn't need to be strong
I was twelve
I needed to be safe

The Day You Went Away

-

January Ninth
It was cold
The day you went away
I felt my heart breaking
And I couldn't breathe
Nothing made sense
The day you went away
I saw your lifeless body
For the first and last time
You weren't hurting anymore
The day you went away
Up the hill
Six feet under
The bell in your casket
The day you went away

Consent.

-
The bonfire was supposed to be
Fun
I mentioned it to my mother
Fun
It was my birthday
Fun
We drove off
Into the sunset
But there was no
Bonfire
There was no
Fun
As you undressed me
Waist down
You ripped away

My life
Just getting started
Only to end
College
Only a million miles away
Never to begin
I said
No
I said
Stop
But you never listened
You kept going
And going
And going
Police questioned my
Dignity
Never to return

Lies.

-
Knife to the heart
Blade to the wrist
She's dead
You said
As I stood there breathing
Funeral plans
Never to happen
I stood there
Breathing
Dead
You said

Lies Pt 2.

-
Chewed up and
Spit out
You put it out
Into the universe
They ripped her clothes
Off
Into the abyss
She said stop
She fought
Scratching
Screaming for
Help
They found DNA
Only to happen
Years later
Lies
Manifested into the
Abyss

Pierre.

-
You'd only come out
To play
When it was most
Dangerous
A distraction?
Maybe
But you saved me
Through the
Screaming
Yelling
Throwing things
Glass breaking
You saved me
Playing tag
Hide and seek
And playing house

In a broken home
You rode a unicycle
Your name was
Pierre
The French boy
Only I could see
Dreaming
Wishing
Twenty years later
You would come back
And save me again
Ashes to ashes and
Dust to dust
Still hoping
You'd come back
One
Last
Time

BPD.

-
Everything is so
Black and white
When it's good
It's great
But
When it's bad
It's horrible
The best thing to happen to me
My worst downfall
I hate you
Don't leave me
I love you so
Leave me alone
To die
I wonder why
They call it
Borderline
As if there was
Even a line
To begin with

Warning Label.

Warning Labels

They come on bottles

Of Poison

Bags

Of Cocaine

Jars

Of Marijuana

Laced pills

Of Fentanyl

But never

You

Or

Me

Petals.

-

He loves me
He loves me not
I said
As I picked off the
Very best parts
Of me
Just so that
You would
Love me

Halloween.

-
Samhain was my
Favorite
Time of year
I get to
Dress up
As something
I am not
And I get away with it
For a night
Everyone wouldn't
Speculate or
Judge or
Complain about
What might have
Been wrong with me
Only to admire
What I truly
Wasn't

Blinded Rage.

-
Twenty years to show for
And it only took
One moment
To unravel it all
Paper on fire
Turning to ash
All I saw was
Red
Until I was
Blinded by rage
Too far gone
To be saved
From the abyss
You know as
Gaslight Kingdom

Forgive Me Father.

Forgive me Father
For I have sinned
I'm broken down and
My wings are pinned
On the inside
You cannot see
What the demons
Have done to me
My skull intact
My brain's a mess
You'd never have guessed
All of the stress
The sticks
And the stones
They never
Broke my bones
But words
Cut like knives alone

Friends.

-
I was their friend
But they weren't mine
Words spoken
No energy exchanged
I was their friend
But they weren't mine
Empty promises
They didn't even try
I was their friend
But they weren't mine
Be the bigger person
People have lives
I was their friend
But they weren't mine
Taken advantage of
Nobody cares anyways
I was their friend
Until I wasn't
They never were mine

Espresso.

-
They say
More espresso
Less depresso
But now
I'm just
Fast
And
Sad

But Daddy.

-

Daddy Daddy
Where are you now
It's been years
I haven't heard from you
Daddy Daddy
Last I heard
You were in the hospital
From all the alcohol
I guess it finally got to you
Daddy Daddy
Why did you leave
You broke mommy's mirror
And hit my boyfriend's car
Daddy Daddy
Did your demons win?
Were the drugs too strong?
Were the voices too loud?

Daddy Daddy
If only
You could see me now
I moved on and
I moved out
I moved up in the world
Daddy Daddy
You're so far gone
You don't know left from right
Or why you even left
Will always be a mystery to me
Maybe the drugs were too much
Maybe the voices were too loud
You got caught up
And now you can't come down
Cloud Nine isn't paradise
Like Heaven and
It's Hell

Grounding Exercise.

-
Name something you can
Hear
Smell
Taste
Feel
And see
I hear you screaming
I smell the downpour of rain
I taste the blood
I feel the abandonment
As I watch you leave
Not knowing
That it would be the last time
I'd ever see you
Under the same roof
Ever
Again
And again
And again
And again

Phases.

-
Like the moon
I know
I will go through phases
But
I can't help but think
That life
Was never supposed to
Be this way
This hard
And
This unforgiving

Heartbreak.

-
Such a term
As heartbreak
Your heart can't break
Muscle and tendon
Don't break
But
They tear
They rip
And eventually
They stop beating
Such a term
As heartbreak

Sticks & Stones.

-
Sticks and stones
May break my bones
But words will
Always
Hurt me
Bones heal
Psychological wounds
Haunt you
Til the
Grave
Ash to ash
And
Dust to dust
Bones heal
Words
Don't

The Encyclopedia Of Mania.

-

The only disorder
To ever cause
A sliver of
Happiness
Mania
They say money
Can't buy happiness
But what is it
Really worth
Another dollar spent
Another bump
Another relationship mangled
Was it really
Worth it?

A Cry For Help.

-
One cut
Two cuts
Three cuts
And four
How many more
Until the sun sets on
Forever
Until the flowers quit blooming
Until the world stops spinning
Until the stars stop shining
How many more
Until the sun sets on
Forever
Until the sun
Sets
On
Forever

Eighteen.

-
Being twenty-four is
So bittersweet
Since
I never thought
I'd make it past
Eighteen

11:51 PM.

-
There are
Nine minutes until
Midnight
A new day
A new beginning
Yet
I'm stuck here
And now
It's 11:51 pm
There are nine minutes
Until midnight
New possibilities
New opportunities
Yet
I'm stuck in
Nine minutes
Until
Midnight

Air.

-

Who knew
The thing that
Kept me alive is what
I'm slowly
Drowning in

Tragedy.

-
Oh what tragedy there is
In a girl
Who loves everything
Under the sun
Except
Herself
She picks
Flowers
Because they are beautiful
But hates herself
Because she is not

Drowning.

-

I lift you up
Just for you
To pull me under
Down beneath the waves
Of insecurity
A tsunami of sadness
An ocean of obscurity
You drag me under
Just so you
Could breathe
Now I'm dorwning
Beneath the waves
Of my very own
Thoughts

Madness.

Was it you
Was it me
Who was mad at who?

Nicotine.

-
Roofied inhales
And
Intoxicated exhales
All for what?
So you feel a little
Less
And relax a little
More
And eventually
It consumes you
Before you can
Consume it
First

Eggshells.

-
Don't you dare
Walk on eggshells
Around me
Save yourself
You'll only
Cut yourself
Picking up my
Broken pieces
Sew me back together
Not before
Pricking yourself
First
Now you're wishing
You had
Gloves

Bullet.

-

He said
I would take a
Bullet
For you
Little did I know
He was the one
Standing behind
The gun
Pulling
The trigger

Death.

-
I pulled a card
And what do you know
It was
Death
Something I had been
Dreaming of
Since I was born
Transformation and endings
Maybe it's finally
My time
Maybe it's not
Only divine intervention
Knows

Brave.

-

You are so brave
For all that you endure
You keep pushing
The flower that blooms
Even in winter

Mama.

God's strongest soldier
He sent to be my
Mama
She taught me
Grace
That too much
Is never enough
My protector
My first best friend
The strongest woman
I've ever had the pleasure of knowing
He sent his strongest soldier
To be my mama
Ashes to ashes and
Dust to dust
I know I'll find you
In another life
And I'd pick you
Over and
Over
To be my mama
Again

Eden.

-

If Eve had never
Bitten the forbidden fruit
If Adam had never
Followed suit
I wonder what the
Gates of Heaven
Would look like
Maybe not so far
Away

Oceans & Puddles.

-
I would have
Traveled oceans for you
Yet
You wouldn't jump puddles
For me

It Wasn't Supposed To Be This Way.

-
Life
Wasn't supposed to be
This way
Babe
Your hands never touched
My throat
I never ran away
Into the dark
Tripping over uneven
Concrete
I still have the scars
To this day
Life was never supposed to
Be this way
I would be up north
Studying humans
You'd be in jail
By now

I'd forgive but
Never forget
What you did or
How you made me feel but
Everything happens for a reason
Right?
Tell me I'm
Wrong
Please
Tell me I'm wrong
I would hate to think
That life
Was never
Supposed to be like
This

Do I?

-
Do I
Stay or
Do I
Go
Twenty years of us
The good and
The bad
I could forget but
I could never forgive
Do I
Run away and
Save myself
Years of agony and
Misery
Floats down the halls of
The house
We once called "home"
Do I
Stay or

Do I
Go
I had to save
My babies
Before I could have ever
Saved you
I can't undo
The past
But I can rewrite
Their future
One without an
Absent father
I chose them
Over you
And unknowingly saved
Myself

Twenty-two.

-
A year after
I was legal
That's when I saw you
Laying in the hospital bed
Stage three
Throat burned
And I couldn't believe
How did we get here
How did you
Get here
Laying with an IV
In your arm

Asking for morphine
So you couldn't feel
Imagine that
A drug that makes you feel
Nothing
When I could feel
Everything all at once
I was there
Watching you fade out
But you were nowhere
To be found

This book was made possible
because of those who
never stopped believing
in me.

Thank you mom.

I love you.

Born and raised in Southeastern Michigan, Brittany enjoys writing poetry as a means to heal in her journey with trauma. When she is not writing, she loves spending time with family, listening to gospel music, and loves playing with her cats, Mirabel and Honey.

Milton Keynes UK
Ingram Content Group UK Ltd.
UKHW030749121124
451094UK00013B/848